The Essential

ROBBEN ISLAND

Harriet Deacon

MAYIBUYE BOOKS
University of the Western Cape, Bellville

DAVID PHILIP PUBLISHERS
Cape Town

The Essential

First published 1997 in southern Africa by David Philip
Publishers (Pty) Ltd, 208 Werdmuller Centre, Claremont
7700 and Mayibuye Books, University of the Western
Cape, Private Bag X17, Bellville 7535

ISBN 0-86486-347-0

Mayibuye History and Literature Series No. 84

Printed in South Africa by National Book Printers,
Drukkery Street, Goodwood, Western Cape

CONTENTS

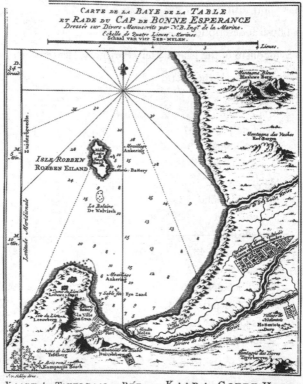

CARTE de la BAYE de la TABLE
et RADE du CAP de BONNE ESPERANCE
Dressée sur Divers Manuscrits par N.B. Ing.r de la Marine.

Echelle de Quatre Lieues Marines
Schaal van vier Zee-Mylen

Montagne Bleue Blaawe Berg

Montagne des Vaches Koe-Bergen

ISLE ROBBEN
ROBBEN EILAND

Mouillage Ankering

Battterie Battery

La Balaine
De Walvisch

Rivier d'Eau douce Zoete Rivier

Zuiderbreedte

Latitude Méridionale

Mouillage Ankering

Sable fin Fyn Zand

Tête du Lion Leeuwenkop

Battery

La Ville Kaap Stad

Fort

Moulin Molen

Village d'Hottentots Hottentot Dorp

Riviere de Sel Zout Rivier

Montagne de la Table Tafelberg

Montagne du Diable Duivelsberg

Bois rond Kompanie Bosch

Montagne des Tigres Tigerbergen

KAART der TAFELBAAI en RÉE van KAAP de GOEDE HOOP,
Geschikt op verscheide Handschriften, door N.B. Ingen.r des Franssen Zeevaards.

A Short History

Most people know Robben Island as the terrible prison of apartheid, where many of South Africa's current leaders were held after 1960. The Island has a long history of imprisonment, but its story also reveals many other connections with South Africa's past, its present and its future.

For the first two centuries after Bartholomeu Dias rounded the Cape of Storms in 1488, Robben Island was used as a pantry, to feed the sailors on passing ships, as a postbox for their letters and, occasionally, as a prison for miscreant sailors. During the period of Dutch rule at the Cape, 1652–1806 (with a brief interlude of British rule between 1795 and 1803), the Island continued to be used as a pantry but it also became increasingly important as a prison, mainly for Cape residents, both black and white, on criminal sentences and for political prisoners from the East Indies. It was during this period that there began the commercial exploitation of the Island's non-food resources: limestone and shells for lime-burning and stone and slate for building.

Under the British after 1806 the Island was again used as a prison, housing soldiers under sentences of transportation or banishment, Cape residents on criminal sentences who were considered particularly dangerous, and political prisoners from the frontiers of the growing colony. The Island also occasionally housed quarantine cases (for the authorities were very afraid of introducing measles or smallpox into the colony) and a few insane people, mainly those who could not be controlled by their families or kept in the small and rickety country jails.

In 1846, however, the prison on Robben Island was closed and the prisoners sent to mainland convict stations to do hard labour. In the old prison buildings the colonial government set up a hospital, called the General Infirmary, which was divided into three sections, housing 'chronic sick', 'lunatics' and 'lepers'. These three institutions closed in 1891, 1921 and 1931 respectively. While it acted mainly as a hospital during the nineteenth century, Robben Island also accommodated a small number of political prisoners, mainly from the eastern and northern frontiers of the colony, and, after 1866, convicts on hard labour sentences who did manual work for the hospital.

After the last 'lepers' left in 1931, the Island stood empty until the outbreak of the Second World War. In 1939 troops were sent there to guard the entrance to Table Bay. When the war ended in 1945 the garrison was reduced. A Coast Artillery School operated there from 1946. The South African Marine Corps controlled the Island from 1951 and in 1955 the South African Navy took charge of what was now known as *S.A.S. Robbeneiland*.

In 1959, however, it was decided that the Island should be taken over by the Prisons Department. From 1961 to 1991 the Island was the site of a maximum security prison, housing those political prisoners considered most threatening to the apartheid government, including South Africa's current President, Nelson Mandela. Now it is a museum, run by the Department of Arts and Culture rather than a prison run by Correctional Services. Its environment is carefully monitored and protected, its symbolic, cultural and historical importance everywhere acknowledged.

A party landing on the island in the late 1800s (Cape Archives)

Robben Island drawn by G.M. Smith c. 1860, a 'lunatic' patient on the island (South African Library)

Physical Description

The Island is actually the summit of an ancient, now sub-merged mountain, linked by an undersea saddle to the Blouberg. Its lower strata are of Malmesbury shale, which form a rocky and somewhat inhospitable coastline. Above this lies a thick limestone and calcrete deposit covered by windblown sands and shell fragments. The rock formations are similar to those of the mainland except that on Robben Island the stratification is nearly horizontal or gently undulating.

The Island is low-lying: the highest point at Minto's Hill (named after a nineteenth-century Surgeon-Superintendent of the General Infirmary) is only 24 metres above sea level. The climate is Mediterranean, as in nearby Cape Town, but the Island experiences stronger wind and colder winters. The Island has a few wells, which were first used by passing sailors in the fifteenth century, though the water is rather brackish. With increasing numbers of people living on the Island in the twentieth century, it became necessary to consider alternative sources of water. Today, water is transported by a cargo ferry boat from the mainland to a reservoir at the Island's harbour.

The Island's inhospitable coastline and the submerged rocks that lie around it have taken many ships by surprise over the years. In a government survey conducted in 1992 of the shipwrecks on the coast of the Island, it was established that at least 22 ships are known to have sunk there,

10 of which were British, 3 Dutch and 3 American. Wreckage from 10 of these ships was located and positively identified. Most of the wrecks occurred on the western or windward side of the Island, which has a jagged rocky profile.

The first reported shipwreck near Robben Island was that of the *Yeanger* of Horne, weighing 900 tons, which was wrecked on the northern shore in 1611 in its search for train oil from seals. No traces of the *Yeanger* remain today, however. Unfortunately, too, one of the other early wrecks, that of the wooden *Dageraad*, carrying silver, which sank in 1694, has probably disintegrated with time. The *Bernicia*, a British barque, sank in 1861 carrying mahogany, 25 kegs of butter, five pianofortes, wines, spirits and other cargo, some of which was salvaged at the time. Apparently one of the 'lunatics' on the Island later died from drinking too much of the spirits he recovered from the wreck. The *Natal*, a Norwegian steam whaler, sank on the north coast in 1914. The *Rangatira*, a British steam liner carrying general cargo, whisky and some domestic animals, foundered on the western coast of the Island in 1916. More recent wrecks include the *Goel no.1* (1976), which was surveying the offshore oil potential along the Cape coast, and the *Daeyang Family*, a Korean vessel carrying iron ore, which sank in 1986.

The types of flora and fauna on Robben Island have been greatly altered by human involvement. Alien plants (such as Rooikrans, Manatoka and Eucalyptus varieties) and animals (such as sheep and cattle, pheasants, rabbits, deer) were introduced and the indigenous plants and animals have consequently been reduced in number or eliminated from the site. But these indigenous forms were fortunately not unique to the Island, the plants being similar to those found in the Strandveld of the West Coast from Cape Point to the Olifants River and the animals mainly penguins and seals. Penguins, which had been eliminated from the Island shores by the nineteenth century, began to return in the early 1980s but the seals have taken longer to re-establish a colony here.

The built environment of the Island has been carefully researched by Patricia Riley for the National Monuments Council. She suggests that the earliest identifiable sites of human occupation are the stone quarry in the south and the lime quarry towards the centre of the Island, which were probably used in Van Riebeeck's time. The account of the Island by the Danish ship's surgeon Cortemunde in 1672 reveals that there were already buildings to accommodate 'many slaves' and 'sometimes 30 to 50 soldiers', with gardens behind them, a 'huge lime-burner' and a flag flying from the signal hill (now called Minto's Hill). Gordon's annotated panorama of 1777 shows an even bigger settlement, situated at the northern end of the Island (later called Murray's Bay after a British whaler who was allowed to live on the Island in 1806), consisting of the *'Posthouder's huis'* (Postholder's house) flanked by long low buildings for the *'bannediten'* (convicts) on the left and utility buildings such as a smithy on the right. The soldiers were accommodated in a line of small houses with vegetable gardens to the north of this, and the slave gardens were situated further away. The caretaker of the signal fire and flag on the hill had a small house and garden there.

The Postholder's house and the convict barracks in the north-east of the Island were used by the whaler John Murray from 1806 to 1823. Between 1806 and 1808 a new settlement was built at the southern end of the Island as a British prison. In 1833 this settlement included a large house for the Commandant, officers' and soldiers' barracks, overseers' houses (one of which was roofed with whale bones), a bakery, butcher and smithy, workshops and prison accommodation for over 200 prisoners. During the early 1840s a church, doctor's residence and parsonage were added. All these buildings were used by the General Infirmary or hospital after 1846. Prisoners kept on the Island after 1846 were housed in huts and makeshift dwellings at Murray's Bay in the northern part of the Island. A lighthouse was built on Minto's Hill in 1863–4. During the 1890s there was an upsurge in building activity to accommodate an increasing number of 'lepers' on the Island. Many of these buildings were destroyed or abandoned during the 1930s.

Extensive building activity again took place on the Island in 1939 and 1940: 150 000 tons of building material were transported to the Island in the former year. The present harbour at Murray's Bay was constructed then, unfortunately destroying obvious traces of the early Dutch buildings. Gun emplacements, underground magazines, plotting rooms and observations towers, quarters for the garrison and two coastal batteries were also built. Many of these buildings are still on the Island today. When the Department of Prisons took over the management of the Island in 1960, further building activity took place – a maximum security and an ordinary criminal prison were built and staff quarters were expanded. In spite of all these changes, however, traces of the more distant history of the Island remain even today in the quarries and the village buildings.

If you drive or walk through the village you can see the leper church, designed by Herbert Baker and built in 1895; the old parsonage; and the English church built in 1841. The present school has a long history: once a lime-house, it was used as a hospital ward from 1846 – the Flagstaff ward – and then became the clubhouse for hospital staff. The guest house, built in 1895 and now restored, used to be the hospital commissioner's house. Next door is the old Dutch Reformed Church parsonage, which was built at the same time.

Prisoners breaking stone in the courtyard of Robben Island Prison in the mid-1960s (Mayibuye Centre)

Symbolism of the Island

Robben Island has always been a powerful element within the symbolic geography of the Cape and of South Africa as a whole. Various groups of people during its history have regarded it as Heaven, Hell or, occasionally, Purgatory. The Island's symbolic value has been heightened because of the shroud of mystery that its natural isolation and the official restriction on access have cast around it over the past four hundred years.

In general the moral weight of its symbolism has not been equally distributed between good and evil. Until the 1990s, Robben Island was most often represented as Hell – a place of banishment from which no one would return. Oliver Tambo commented in 1980, 'The tragedy of Africa, in racial and political terms, [has been] concentrated in the southern tip of the continent – in South Africa, Namibia, and, in a special sense, Robben Island.' Now, however, its strongest symbolism is that of victory over apartheid and other human rights abuses: 'the indestructibility of the spirit of resistance against colonialism, injustice and oppression'. It is, to many, a sign of the nation's maturity, of the Rainbow Nation having reached the democratic nirvana.

The Image of Hell

The image of Robben Island as a democratic paradise draws much of its energy from inverting the old negative symbolism. Revisiting the representation of the Island as Hell can help us to understand its current meaning in South African society. Hell has physical as well as symbolic dimensions: as the critic Jacobs has said, 'Topologically and symbolically Robben Island has always represented the ultimate margin to which the Pretoria Government banished its opposition.' The Island's role as a place of secure banishment was cemented in Cape mythology as early as the seventeenth century. But it was also a place to which the misfits of society were sent: it was used for quarantine cases, the chronic sick, 'lepers' and 'lunatics' during most of the nineteenth century. For those in power, banishment of such people to the Island represented a symbolic cleansing of the southern African subcontinent.

As for those sent to the Island under these terms, resistance to banishment was often more than simply a statement against their imprisonment: it was also a symbolic gesture against their definition as people unworthy of inclusion in South African society. For example, while on the Island a Muslim leader in the eighteenth century transcribed an important legal text which he was later to use in encouraging the development of a subculture of resistance among Muslims in Cape Town. Political and criminal prisoners in the early nineteenth century plotted a mass escape. Lepers in the late nineteenth century organised a programme of resistance to improve the conditions under which they were detained on the Island. Political prisoners in the period after 1961 drew on one another's strengths and skills, transcending the boundaries of their various political affiliations, and were able to negotiate for better conditions, including the right to study by correspondence. These residents in particular were able to challenge the dominant symbol of the Island as a 'hell-hole' by also making it into a 'university'.

The Image of Purgatory

Occasionally, Robben Island has been represented as the middle ground between Heaven and Hell, a place of waiting called Purgatory. The historian Nigel Penn has suggested that, for the early European visitors to the Cape, Dante's 'Isle of Purgatory' was in fact Robben Island, situated at the foot of the Paradise of Table Mountain, and separated from it by a dangerous crossing of icy water. For prisoners on transportation sentences the Island prison was true Purgatory: a halfway point between the Cape and the feared convict settlements of Van Diemen's Land or New South Wales.

The Image of Heaven

There have been two major moments in the history of the Island in which it has come to symbolise that which is positive rather than negative about South Africa. These

---

Overleaf: A leper ward in the early 1900s (Cape Archives)

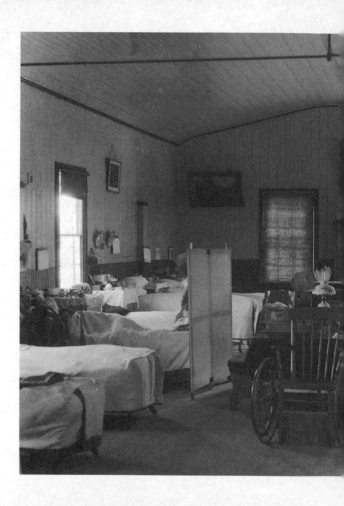

moments of redefinition both occurred at times when new governments sought to emphasise their moral modernity, specifically before an international audience, and to construct a new source of national pride. The first moment was during the mid-nineteenth century when an emerging Cape Town middle class wished to earn self-rule from Britain. The second was during the recent transition to democracy. As a positive symbol, the Island is now thought of mainly as a site for the *spiritual* and *moral* regeneration of the nation. In the past, on the other hand, it was considered an ideal site for people's *physical* regeneration.

At present the Island is seen as a place symbolising the triumph over apartheid; this image is linked to a reformulation of national identity based on a particular view of modernity (represented by the discourse of 'human rights'). A similar positive reformulation of the Island's role occurred during the mid-nineteenth century. At this time Cape colonists wanted to transform the Robben Island lunatic asylum from a backward-looking place of punishment into a modern curative institution. In this new form it would stand as a symbol of the humanitarianism, modernity and maturity of the colony, which wanted more political autonomy from Britain. This attempt to transform the Island's image succeeded only briefly. After the granting of self-rule to the Cape in 1872 and the death of the reformist doctor in charge of the asylum in the same year, the white colonists gradually stopped supporting the institution with paying patients and a good press.

In the nineteenth century Robben Island was considered ideal for a hospital because it was both secure (isolating dangerous cases) and healthy (providing a good environment for cure). Its use as a hospital thus fed both on its negative image as a place of banishment (Hell) and on its positive image as healthy (Heaven), being far from the polluting environment of Cape Town.

Throughout most of the nineteenth century miasma theories of disease dominated medical and popular thinking. These theories held that decaying organic matter was the source of foul-smelling emanations, which then produced disease. In crowded towns, as one English commentator put it, thousands 'who know no better ... wallow in the mire and inhale poison at every breath'. Places at some distance from towns were considered more healthy, and islands were particularly recommended as health resorts. A 'change of air' was therefore often prescribed as a cure for chronic disease during the nineteenth century. 'Lepers' in particular were thought to benefit from sea bathing, which improved the condition of their skin, and 'lunatics' from the peace and quiet of a country environment. These ideas made it possible to think of the Robben Island hospitals as places of cure.

During the last few decades of the twentieth century, debates about the future of the Island – as nature reserve, holiday resort and museum – have also represented competing attempts by various political groupings to reformulate the meaning of the Island and its role as a national symbol in a more positive way. Under apartheid rule, proposals to change the Island's image were part of a public relations exercise for the benefit of the international community. The *Cape Argus* explained in 1975 that Robben Island would be 'far pleasanter to point out to guests of the Cape' if it were a nature reserve or holiday resort rather than a prison. In 1981 the newspaper reiterated: 'If (or when) the Island becomes a health resort, Robben Island would be free at last of the stigma that has hung over it for hundreds of years – that of a penal settlement, leper colony and outpost for the insane.'

It was only after 1994, however, when the last political prisoners were released from the Island and a democratic government was elected, that creating a more enduring positive symbolism of the Island became practically possible. But now the Isalnd is not so much a *health* resort as a place for moral and spiritual regeneration – for individuals as well as the nation as a whole.

EXPERIENCES OF THE ISLAND

Many people have now experienced what it is like to be on Robben Island. For about only R80 per adult, members of public have been able to take a trip to the Island on one of the old prison boats, see the village, the prison, the quarries and the penguins, and, for a little extra money (donated to support ex-prisoners), return home with a lump of Robben Island quarry stone authenticated by the President himself. This experience is very powerful for most visitors, both local and foreign, but it does not always help us to understand how people experienced being on the Island in the past. Their experiences were not of course always the same, but neither were they always negative.

Some prison and hospital staff in the last two hundred years have left testimony of how they loved being on the Island, where time was often spent fishing and having picnics among the spring flowers. Some of those who served the apartheid prison during the last thirty years are now employed in the Robben Island Museum and are very happy to be able to stay in their former home. Living on the Island seems to give people in general the pleasant feeling that they are special, closer to the sea that defines the city, closer to nature, and now residing in the symbolic heart of the nation.

A feeling of community also developed among the political prisoners sent there after 1960. But living on the Island in chains, physical or otherwise, naturally provided a total-

ly different set of experiences for residents. It was physically and emotionally debilitating to be ill-treated by prison
guards and to be separated from friends and family. At the
same time, for many of the anti-apartheid prisoners, life on
the Island provided an opportunity to study, to meet their
leaders and to discuss political issues.

TELLING THE STORY OF ROBBEN ISLAND THROUGH ITS RESIDENTS

Autshumato

Autshumato (also called Autshumao, and named Harry or Herry by the Europeans) was a Khoikhoi leader who became an interpreter for Europeans passing by the Cape after 1631 and an intermediary between them and the Khoikhoi once a Dutch settlement was established in 1652. He was taken to Java by the English in 1631–2 and, after his return to the Cape, was said to speak 'a little English'. His association with Robben Island probably began in 1632 when he asked passing sailors to ferry him and twenty of his followers to the Island. There the group remained, on and off, for the next eight years, protected from their mainland Khoikhoi enemies and within easy reach of the Island's edible resources, which included penguins and seals.

On the Island Autshumato acted as postman for European ships passing the Cape on their way to trade with the East Indies; he would signal with fires from the top of what is now called Minto's Hill, where the lighthouse is situated. Mundy's account of a visit to the Island in 1634 reveals that Autshumato was dressed in 'English habit from head to foote'; he and his now augmented band of followers, sixty in all, lived in seven 'little Cottages'. By 1640, this group, and no doubt passing sailors as well, had exhausted

---

Overleaf: Khoi bartering sheep with Dutch sailors (SAL)

much of the natural flora and fauna on the Island, and Autshumato and his followers returned to the mainland.

Back on the mainland, Autshumato was instrumental in helping the Dutch settlers barter with the Khoikhoi for cattle after the Cape Town refreshment station was established in 1652. Autshumato was to return to Robben Island in 1658, however, as a prisoner: as the Dutch put it, 'the ex-interpreter, or, as the English used to call him, King Harry, was removed ... from his kingdom in this furthest corner of Africa to the Robben Island'. Van Riebeeck had contemplated this step as early as 1652, when negotiations between the Dutch and Khoi were not progressing sufficiently well for his liking. Autshumato's former associations with the English did not help matters. In 1658 the Island postholder, Rijck Overhagen, received orders that Autshumato and his two fellow prisoners were to be given a little tobacco if they helped herd the sheep, but that they had to search for the rest of their food.

After a year and a half on the Island, Autshumato and a fellow prisoner managed to steal a little rowing-boat and escape from the Island. Their boat was found about two weeks afterwards by the Dutch: the latter could not believe that the men had survived the difficult crossing. It was only a year later that Autshumato applied to live near the Castle again and resumed his role as interpreter. He died in 1663.

Krotoa

Krotoa (whom the Dutch called Eva) was apparently Autshumato's niece, the daughter of his sister, but it is hard to be sure of the nature of the blood relationship between them as Khoikhoi family terms did not always match those of the Dutch commentators.

Her first contact with the Dutch was, however, as a domestic worker or, perhaps more descriptively, an unpaid servant. She was about ten when she was brought into the Van Riebeeck household, soon after their arrival, and here she began to learn Dutch. Her skill in this language soon impressed the family; by 1657 she was being used as an interpreter. By 1660, Krotoa had edged out her uncle as the principal interpreter for the Dutch settlement at the Cape. She was baptised in the Dutch Reformed Church two years later and by 1664 she had married a prominent member of the Dutch colony, the junior surgeon Pieter van Meerhoff. In 1660 she was described as fluent in Dutch and reasonably competent in Portuguese. Apart from various periods of absence to stay with family members, she remained at the Castle until her husband became superintendent of the Robben Island prison in 1665.

Van Meerhoff's job at Robben Island was, as the historian Candy Malherbe says, not a plum post. He had a number of time-consuming and difficult tasks, including the monitoring of ships entering the bay, the supervision of convicts who collected shells for lime and stone for the building of the Castle, the control of a small garrison and the tending of a flock of sheep. For Krotoa, isolated from her family, the sojourn on the Island could not have been a particularly happy one. A doctor was called to her aid in 1667 for a condition that seems to have been related to over-consumption of alcohol.

After her husband was killed on a slaving and trading expedition to Mauritius and Madagascar, Krotoa was allowed to return to the mainland in September 1668. Soon afterwards reports were made by the Dutch of her allegedly drunken and adulterous behaviour, and she left the Castle and her two children for the more friendly Khoikhoi kraals. In February 1669, however, she was imprisoned at the Castle and banished to Robben Island, this time as a prisoner. She died in 1674. The Dutch described her on her death as 'this brutal aboriginal, [who] was always still hovering between' the Dutch and Khoikhoi cultures, yet she was given a Christian burial in the Castle.

Pieter de Neyn

One of the earliest visitors to the Island wrote a poem about it. He was Pieter de Neyn, sent to the Cape in 1671 by the Dutch East India Company to become fiscal (a judicial officer). After some dispute over his fitness for the role of fiscal (he was thought on arrival at the Cape to have been involved in smuggling goods from the East Indies to Holland), his appointment was finalised and he was asked to inspect conditions at the Robben Island prison, where he stayed from 8 to 12 September 1674. Here he was to write one of six poems dealing with his experiences in Cape Town. He found the main house on the Island threatened by drifting sand and commented more on this and on the inhospitable nature of the Island than on the prison itself. What follows is the poem about his visit to Robben Island, translated by Professor Roy Pheiffer:

'Being on Robben Island, having been sent by the Council as Commissioner to establish some order amongst a set of prisoners'

I may well be on the Land of Seals [*robbe*],
Manned by a population of stupid roguery,
Where no provision for the throat or the tooth,
Or against the sharp Cold is made,
Sent as a Signor deputy;
But should I reach the firm land again,
This I swear by the highest Saint,
And give my right hand upon it,

And also my word and honour as pledge,
(Unless something's amiss with my head)
That no one will ever plant me there;
For know that I am of such a type,
Who likes to be a regular customer,
Where sadness is totally banned,
And glasses filled right to the rim,
And you merrily sit around with pipes, 'cos
I still sing in my same old fashion,
I shove this Island to one side,
And will have nothing to do with its arid sand.

Muslim leaders

Robben Island played an important part in the establishment of a Muslim community in South Africa. East Indian political prisoners were sent to the Island from the late seventeenth century until the late eighteenth century. Sayyed Aloeurie, or Alawie (Tuan Said), imprisoned there in 1744 and released in 1761, became the first imam of the Cape Town Muslim community. Tuan Guru, a prince from Tidore in the Ternate Islands, was imprisoned on the Island between 1780 and 1793, thereafter becoming the first chief imam in Cape Town. While on the Island he wrote an important work on Islamic philosophy. Many other Muslims were also imprisoned on the Island by the Dutch during the eighteenth century.

A commemorative shrine to men like these has been erected on the Island, near the prison buildings. The shrine is for Cape Muslims also a 'memorial to freedom, a symbol of their religious struggle, and an indication of the wonder of Islam', according to the historian Achmat Davids. As he points out, it is ironic that this modern building was erected by the prison authorities, in 1960. Cape Muslims have been visiting the site since the nineteenth century, if not before, however, and the *karamat* forms part of a group of important Islamic religious sites in the Cape Peninsula. Nigel Penn suggests that the shrine honours Sheikh Madura (also known as the King, Prince, Pangeran or Raja of Madura), who was banished to the Island in the 1740s and died there in 1754. His body was returned to his son and now lies buried in Jakarta.

It is therefore not certain exactly which eighteenth-century political prisoners *are* buried beneath the shrine. Oral history favours a prisoner called Tuan Matarah, who is thought to have been a holy man who attended to the other prisoners' medical and spiritual needs. But Davids suggests that the person most likely to be buried in the grave at the shrine was actually called Hadji Matarim rather than Matarah. Described as a 'Mohammedan Priest' in the prison records, he was banished in chains to the Island in 1744 with Sayyed Aloeurie and died there the following year.

David Stuurman

David Stuurman was a Khoi leader from the Eastern Cape who was imprisoned on Robben Island in 1809 and 1819 and banished to New South Wales for attempting escape from the Island in 1820. Stuurman had been the central figure in an experiment on the eastern frontier of the colony: here the Batavian government of 1803–6 allowed some Khoi to establish a settled community in order to restore peace on the frontier and separate them from the Xhosa with whom they had previously allied themselves against the settlers.

Relations between Stuurman's followers and the British deteriorated by 1809 and after allegedly forming an alliance with the Xhosa under Cungwa (Konga), Stuurman and a few others were arrested and sent to Robben Island. Here he met up with a former ally against the colonial government in the third frontier war (1799–1803), Hans Trompetter, who had also been sent there. Stuurman escaped after a year with a few companions, however, and made his way back through the colony to the Eastern Cape where he hid among the Xhosa. In 1819, after fighting on the side of the Xhosa in the fifth frontier war, he was recaptured and rejoined Trompetter on the Island.

Both Trompetter and Stuurman were involved in a daring escape from the Island in 1820. Although the number of prison guards had been increased in 1819, the buildings were still insecure and the locks were worn out. A failed escape attempt in March 1820 was followed by a mass outbreak in August of that year, which the Colonial Secretary ascribed to the 'manifest system of neglect' at the institution. The prisoners who escaped were mainly Khoi and Xhosa, led by the detained prisoner Johan Schmidt and Hans Trompetter. They overpowered the guard and took weapons from the store, leaving eight soldiers wounded. They then stole several of the whaler Murray's boats and set off for the mainland. Only one of the three boats landed safely at Blouberg Strand, however, and several of the occupants of the capsized boats drowned.

Two of the survivors of the subsequent shootout with the authorities managed to elude capture – the Khoi prisoners Abraham Leendert and Kieviet. The rest were rounded up and convicted of 'mutiny and open violence with arms' in Cape Town. The leaders of the escape, Schmidt and Trompetter, were hanged and decapitated, and their heads displayed on iron spikes at Robben Island. David Stuurman was treated more leniently because he had saved the life of Murray's overseer during the escape. He was sent in 1823 to New South Wales, where he died seven years later.

Makhanda

Among those who drowned at Blouberg Strand in the escape of 1820 was the Xhosa leader Makhanda. Makhanda, also called 'Nxele' or 'Links' (meaning 'left-handed' in Xhosa and Afrikaans respectively), was a Xhosa warrior-prophet, who renounced his Christian upbringing and became a strong advocate of Xhosa tradition among the Ndlambe. The Ndlambe (H'lambie) and the Ngqika (Gaika) were sub-groups of the Rharhabe clan of Xhosa, which had been formed by a split within the original Xhosa clan, the Gcaleka.

In the frontier war of 1818–19 Makhanda led an unsuccessful attack by combined Gcaleka and Ndlambe forces on Grahamstown. This gave the colonists a much-wanted excuse to drive them across the Keiskamma River. Makhanda surrendered in 1819, wanting to settle for peace as his people were starving, their crops burnt and their stock dying. He was then sent to Robben Island, which soon entered Xhosa mythology as the 'Isle of Makhanda'.

Governor Lord Charles Somerset was at pains to indicate that Makhanda had been detained on Robben Island to provide 'security of his person' and loss of liberty but no other punishment. He was to be given a separate room in the garden of the local whaler and fisherman, John Murray. These privileges were not enough to hold him there, however, and he joined the mass outbreak in 1820. After Makhanda's boat capsized during his escape attempt, legend has it that for a time he clung to a rock, shouting encouragement to others, before he was lost in the surf.

Cape Town's House of Correction for women (Cape Archives)

Abigail Diamond

Abigail Diamond was an Irishwoman who emigrated to Cape Town in the early nineteenth century. She and her husband Michael may have been among a group of Irish labourers who were brought to the Cape in 1823. Many of these people, according to the historian Shirley Judges, sought solace in drink. Irish immigrants were at the bottom of the social ladder among settlers in Cape Town and had to take the most menial jobs. For these people, and other poor groups in the town, drinking provided a relatively cheap form of recreation and escape. Abigail Diamond was one of those who could not withstand the temptations of alcohol, and spent much of her life in and out of the House of Correction (the jail for women in Cape Town) for disorderly conduct and drunkenness. She was also involved in the sex trade in Cape Town, which was dominated in the 1830s by those called 'Bastard Hottentots' (of Khoi and European ancestry) and by Irishwomen. Her activities, which fitted the negative stereotype of Irish immigrants as drunk and immoral, made Abigail Diamond a figure of notoriety in Cape Town.

It is therefore not surprising that she was admitted to the Robben Island chronic sick wards in 1848. She was in fact one of many British and Irish immigrants sent to the Island during the next forty years alongside ex-slaves and poor black Capetonians. Little is known of them except that they could not provide for themselves in sickness and old age and had consequently to rely on the reluctant support of the colonial government.

Maqoma photographed in the early 1860s (SAL)

Maqoma

Several Xhosa chiefs came as prisoners to Robben Island in 1858 after the Cattle Killings of 1856–7. The Cattle Killings were a millenarian Xhosa offensive against encroaching British rule, which nearly destroyed the Xhosa themselves, as cattle were slaughtered and crops not planted. Among those imprisoned on Robben Island was Maqoma.

Born in 1798, Maqoma (or Macomo) was a son of the Xhosa chief Ngqika. Maqoma has been misrepresented as a drunken troublemaker and cattle thief who masterminded an unprovoked irruption into the colony in 1834 and eventually led his subjects into the 'irrational' Cattle Killing catastrophe. On the contrary, argues the historian Timothy Stapleton, he was one of the most important nineteenth-century Xhosa leaders, considered even by his British opponents as a formidable tactician, a masterly politician and a brilliant orator. He placated European raiders with cattle tribute in the 1820s and 1830s, and only retaliated against the British in 1834 after he had been forced off his land three times. He could not have been a confirmed alcoholic, says Stapleton, as he sustained successful guerrilla insurgency tactics during the frontier war of 1850–3. He drank mainly at meetings with colonial officials, who deliberately plied him with alcohol to try to befuddle his judgement. He supported the Cattle Killing only after it had become such a powerful movement that failure to do so would have threatened his chiefly power and prestige.

Maqoma and his wife Katyi were banished to Robben

Island after he was convicted in 1857 of having been a party to the murder of another chief who had refused to destroy his cattle. For the first month of his stay he was put in solitary confinement by Superintendent Minto, who 'was afraid of him by the report [he had] had'. Maqoma raged that he was 'much discontented' about being imprisoned on Robben Island and in 1858 demanded a trial or liberation, but to no avail. His wife, then ill on the Island, was said to have refused medicine, saying, 'No, my heart is sore, I want to die.'

By 1859 there were eight Xhosa leaders on the Island: Maqoma, his brother Xhoxho, Mhala (the son of Ndlambe), Fadana, Kenti, Dilima (the son of Phato, leader of a Khoi–Xhosa clan) and his two younger brothers Umpfafa and Mate. The prisoners had little contact with their relatives. Mhala was fortunate to have a son at the Zonnebloem College in Cape Town, who asked whether he could visit Mhala on Robben Island. Mhala's and Xhoxho's wives, however, refused to come from the Eastern Cape. The prisoners wrote lonely letters home requesting news. Although they received adequate food they were allowed no alcohol. They were, however, able to hunt hares and Cape pheasants on the Island. Their accommodation consisted of huts covered with tarpaulins at Murray's Bay, where they slept first on mattresses on the sand, and then on stretchers.

Other Xhosa captives who had been temporarily imprisoned in Cape Town, including Xayimpi (involved in an attack on Woburn village in the Eastern Cape) and Stokwe, joined the prisoners at Murray's Bay in 1862. They were now given three weather-boarded houses instead of huts, and a few cows, which soon died.

In 1863 Dilima and some others were released. Then on 19 April 1869, the last three prisoners, Maqoma, Siyolo and Xhoxho left the Island by boat. The Rev. Mr Baker, the resident Anglican chaplain on the Island, wrote in his diary that they thanked him on their departure, accepted some small gifts and said they hoped the Bishop would send them a good missionary. They were all allowed to return home, but Maqoma was soon reconvicted. While he had been on the Island, Maqoma's land in the Ciskei, near Fort Beaufort, was taken by the British. After trying to reoccupy his land, he was re-imprisoned on Robben Island in 1871, this time without his wife. He died in the pauper wards, reportedly 'from natural causes', a weak and lonely old man, in September 1873. Praise poems described him as 'a black snake who crosses rivers' and ascribed his death 'on the white people's island' to a gunshot wound inflicted by his white prison guards. There is no contemporary documentary evidence to substantiate the claim that he was murdered, however.

Langalibalele

After Maqoma died in 1873, the Island was empty of political prisoners for barely a year. Then in 1874 the Hlubi chief Langalibalele arrived in rather inauspicious circumstances. Langalibalele, or Mthethwa (1818–89), became the chief of the Hlubi in Natal, one of the most powerful independent black chiefdoms remaining in the country in 1873. The Hlubi had been relocated by Sir Theophilus Shepstone to the upper stretches of the Bushman's River near the Drakensberg in order to form a buffer between the San in the Drakensberg and the colonists. Langalibalele's growing following, and his influence as a visionary, rain-maker and independent leader, began to threaten the colonists and tension rose. But the spark for what became known as the 'Langalibalele Rebellion' in 1873 was the refusal by the Hlubi to register weapons they were bringing back from the diamond fields in Griqualand West. The colonists finally sent troops after Langalibalele, but he escaped to Lesotho. The colonists thereupon disbanded the Hlubi, and confiscated their land and their stock.

Langalibalele was finally arrested in Lesotho, and tried early in 1874. His trial is still regarded today as a major travesty of justice, as his lawyer was not given the assurance that British law would prevail. The lawyer withdrew in protest, and Langalibalele was not represented. He was convicted of treason, murder and rebellion, with trivial support for these accusations. J.W. Colenso, Bishop of Natal, protested in vain against the trial, even going to England to

Langalibalele in captivity (Cape Archives)

plead the case with the Secretary of State for the Colonies.

Langalibalele was, however, banished to Robben Island for life under a special Act of the Cape parliament, called the Natal Criminals Act. Reflecting the general opinion of colonists at the time, the Rev. Baker opined that even though Langalibalele had not been found guilty by *technical* justice, it was better for him to be kept out of harm's way. Colenso continued to fight for redress. After a visit to the Island, he requested that the prisoner be relieved of convict dress and be given a change in diet. Superintendent Biccard replied that he and his son had already been given civilian-style canvas clothing, and that they would now get more bread and meat, and a ration of beer daily. They were not allowed bottles with their beer or wine because their room opened into the convict barracks, and it was feared that they might trade the items with the convicts.

Later in 1875 the Secretary of State, Lord Carnavon, finally succeeded in forcing the Cape parliament to reconsider Langalibalele's sentence. Carnavon felt that lifelong banishment on Robben Island was too severe in relation to the crime committed and he complained also that the trial had been irregular. Parliament grudgingly repealed the Natal Criminals Act and Langalibalele was released from Robben Island in August 1875. Still considered a threat to settler security, he was imprisoned instead on the farm Uitvlugt, near the modern suburb of Pinelands, where Cetshwayo was later to be held in 1879. While at Uitvlugt Langalibalele asked the authorities to fulfil their promise of sending one of his wives down from Natal. He asked his favourite wife, Vokwe (or Voko), to 'go to him, and cook for him and stay with him' but she refused. She said that she did not want to go alone, as she was afraid that 'the Authorities have killed him long ago' and she did not want to be singled out because 'all the Chief wives want to go'. In 1887 Langalibalele was taken back to Natal, where he died two years later.

Franz Jacobs

In about 1887, a man called Franz Jacobs was admitted to the Robben Island leper hospital. A Dutch Reformed Church member and a teacher, he was classified by the Island staff as a 'coloured Afrikander'. He had been living with his wife and seven children in Woodstock. Leprosy, as we now know, is not quite as infectious as tuberculosis, but prior to the development of sulphonamide cures in the 1940s, it was a greatly feared disease. In the Cape Colony during the 1880s there was thought to be a rising epidemic of leprosy, and people were afraid of those suffering from the disease. Worried that his wife would not be able to find a job if he stayed with her, Jacobs went voluntarily to the Island hospital. For the first while he·was able to visit his family in Woodstock occasionally, but after the enforcement of the Leprosy Repression Act in 1892 he and the other lepers were not allowed to leave the Island at all.

Jacobs, who became a teacher and catechist for the lepers, was instrumental in organising protests among black male lepers (patients were segregated by race and sex). The lepers were unhappy about their forced detention on the Island, saying they were 'banished' from society. They felt that the Leprosy Repression Act targeted black lepers and claimed some white lepers were allowed to remain with their families on the mainland (this was probably true). It was often difficult for friends and relatives to visit them, there was only one little room where they could meet visitors, and parcels from friends often failed to reach them.

The lepers said they were 'left on the Island as people who are dead'. They were not permitted to visit the female lepers on the Island. They were forced to work to get tobacco rations, their food was poorly prepared and their clothing inadequate. The parallels with the problems experienced by political prisoners of the post-1960 period are very clear.

The way in which the Island lepers protested against these problems also has echoes in the later period. Jacobs appealed (in anonymous letters smuggled out of the hospital) to the highest judicial and moral authorities: the Colonial Secretary, the Attorney-General and the Queen. He wrote to the Queen saying that as she had freed the slaves in 1834 she should also free the lepers. They were British subjects but did not enjoy their freedoms. Not surprisingly, Jacobs received no reply from her. Prompted by these and other complaints from the lepers, however, the Colonial Secretary visited the Island in August 1892 and restored the tobacco rations to all patients.

Having failed to get satisfaction on all counts, Jacobs then began a campaign taking advantage of the discrepancy between the humanitarian veneer of the Leprosy Repression Act and its essentially punitive application. Perhaps one could compare this to the way in which the apartheid regime was forced to allow prisoners certain rights under international conventions for treating political prisoners. The Leprosy Act, which demanded indefinite and complete segregation of all lepers, was not dealing with criminals. It was actually supposed to hospitalise lepers for treatment and did not lay down rules for leper behaviour or punishment. Jacobs used the tension in the Act between treatment and imprisonment to press for further changes. Under his leadership, the lepers refused treatment by the nurses, demanded luxuries like 'Cruet Stands, Finger Glasses, Table napkins and delicacies' to eat, and threatened to beat up the doctors and rape the women on the Island. The lepers felt they had nothing to lose: Jacobs told the staff he was already a convict.

The resident surgeon, who said that Jacobs 'instead of being pampered deserves the cells', brought in the police, imprisoned Jacobs and sent him to Somerset Hospital where he didn't even have the company of his leper friends. The Cape government hushed up the protest and its repression, and suggested to the British government that Jacobs was insane. Jacobs, unhappy in the Somerset Hospital, withdrew his complaints and said he had been tempted by the Devil to resist. But, embarrassed by the reports in the English press (which fortunately for them did not reach the Cape newspapers), the colonial government introduced improvements to the food (Muslims now received specially prepared meals), issued free passes to visitors and brought in a Dutch Reformed minister for the lepers. A group of MPs visited the Island in July 1893 and published a favourable report in the local papers.

Jacobs was sent back to the Island for a brief period in 1893, but died in the Somerset Hospital later that year. Unlike the political prisoners at Robben Island in the recent past, he did not enjoy the sweet victory of release, nor did he enjoy the smaller victories gained through the protests he had orchestrated in 1892.

Oswald Pirow

Pirow, an advocate who was a prominent supporter of General J.B.M. Hertzog and the Afrikaner nationalist cause, was connected to Robben Island in two major ways. During the Second World War, he was instrumental in turning the Island into an important part of the country's coastal defences; and between 1958 and his death in 1959 he played the role of Crown prosecutor during the Treason Trial of thirty ANC leaders, including Nelson Mandela and Ahmed Kathrada, who were later imprisoned on the Island.

In the 1930s Pirow was a man increasingly attracted to authoritarian and totalitarian principles of government, a particular admirer of Dr Salazar, the iron-fisted ruler of Portugal. His political distance from the British Empire caused him to adopt a fairly neutral stance during the lead-up to the Second World War, and his local affiliations made him more worried about black insurrection than foreign invasion. As early as 1936, however, in his capacity as the Minister of Defence, Railways and Harbours, Pirow recognised the possible utility of the Island as a military base, and reserved it for military use in May of that year. During the next few years, tons of military equipment and building materials were brought onto the Island, and by the 1940s it had changed considerably. Military staff, both black and white, men and women, were brought in to service and operate the equipment and communications. After the war, some Permanent Force staff remained to maintain the equipment and protect Table Bay if needed. In 1959, however, it was announced that the Island would become a maximum security prison.

Although Oswald Pirow died before the famous Rivonia Trial, which sent many prisoners to the Island in 1964, he was involved as prosecutor in the unsuccessful Treason Trial involving many of the same people during the late 1950s. In his autobiography, Mandela describes Pirow as 'a longtime Afrikaner nationalist, and an outspoken supporter of the Nazi cause ... a virulent anti-communist'. His selection as prosecutor showed how concerned the government was to win the case against the anti-apartheid leaders. Brought in during 1958 at the pre-trial stage, Pirow's aggressive involvement 'changed the atmosphere of the trial', and was instrumental in the magistrate's decision that the case for high treason against the accused would be tried in the Supreme Court. He conducted a vigorous attack on the ANC leaders, but on hearing of his death late in the following year Mandela says in his autobiography that while they were grateful that the prosecution was thereby weakened, the accused did not rejoice at his death. He says, 'We had developed a certain affection for our opponent, for despite Pirow's noxious political views, he was a humane man without the violent personal racism of the government he was acting for.'

Robert Sobukwe in his quarters on the Island (New African)

Robert Sobukwe

Robert Mangaliso Sobukwe, founding president of the Pan Africanist Congress, was born in Graaff-Reinet in 1924. His Xhosa first name, 'Mangaliso', means 'man of wonders'. As a student, lay preacher and teacher in the 1940s and 1950s, Sobukwe was an outspoken opponent of apartheid. He lost his student bursaries for speaking out against missionaries and white liberals who, he said, had sown division among the African people. He also lost his first teaching job because he refused to teach the official apartheid history.

Sobukwe's politics were Africanist. Like him, his biographers have been careful to note that this was not a racist politics, as he defined 'Africans' not by the colour of their skin but by their commitment to Africa. Sobukwe was instrumental in the formation of the Pan Africanist Congress in 1959, a breakaway group from the African National Congress, seeking the 'establishment and maintenance of an Africanist socialist democracy'. The PAC differed from the ANC in its refusal to accept any white liberal or communist leadership. It stood for a complete overthrow of the apartheid system, not equality and power-sharing between its proponents and what it called 'true' Africans.

After the Sharpeville massacre in March 1960, in which protesters against the restrictive pass laws were shot by the police, both the PAC and the ANC were banned. Sobukwe was tried for his role in the anti-pass campaign and sentenced to three years in prison. The PAC had a policy of 'no bail, no defence, no fine' as they did not recognise the authority of the apartheid courts, and so he was not defended in court. In 1963, after completion of the three-year sentence, Sobukwe was detained further by a special Act of parliament, and transferred from Pretoria to what was by then becoming the central political prison of the apartheid system, Robben Island. In justifying this unprecedented step, John Vorster, then Minister of Justice and later Prime Minister of the country, said of Sobukwe, 'He is a man with a magnetic personality, great organizing ability and a divine sense of his mission.' Vorster said he intended detaining Sobukwe 'until this side of eternity'. The government was worried that with the rising tide of Africanist militancy, represented by an offshoot of the PAC called Ama-Afrika Poqo ('The real owners of Africa'), or Poqo for short, Sobukwe's release could trigger a massive uprising among Africans.

The special statute under which Sobukwe was detained on the Island, known as the 'Sobukwe Clause', had to be approved annually, which it was until his release from the Island. On the Island, he enjoyed slightly better conditions than the other political prisoners, but he was completely isolated from them. At first he was kept in a house formerly used by a 'coloured' warder (all black warders were removed from the Island in 1963), but later in 1963 he was transferred to a small bungalow which had been part of the 'coloured' school. In this place he grew a small garden, with seeds donated by the Defence and Aid Fund in Cape Town. His pumpkins, squashes and cucumbers grew well, except when water shortages on the Island forced him to stop watering them. He studied by correspondence with the University of London for an economics degree, which he passed in 1968. But his time on the Island was profoundly lonely, its monotony broken only by occasional visits from his wife Veronica and their children, and by the silent salutes of passing prisoners from the main prison. When the other prisoners were marched by, Sobukwe used to go outside and take a handful of the soil from his garden, allowing the sand to run through his fingers, as if to say that nothing mattered more than the recovery of their land.

After Sobukwe's release from the Island – prompted by official fears that years of solitary confinement might permanently damage him psychologically – he was sent to Kimberley, a place where he had never lived before, and kept under house arrest until his death in 1978.

Neville Alexander

Neville Alexander was born in Cradock in the Eastern Cape, in 1936, the son of a teacher and a carpenter. He has said in a recently published interview with Charles Villa-Vicencio that he acquired his iron discipline and principled nature from his father, who advised him, when visiting him in prison on Robben Island, to 'be obedient, but do not lose your dignity'. While studying at the University of Cape Town and in Germany, Alexander became a committed socialist and Trotskyist. He left the Non-European Unity Movement when it rejected his call for guerrilla warfare against the apartheid state in the early 1960s. He formed the Yu Chi Chan Club, to conduct further research into the use of guerrilla warfare, and later the National Liberation Front (NLF) to undertake the violent overthrow of the state. For these activities he was arrested and imprisoned on Robben Island for ten years, from 1964 to 1974.

Alexander describes his experience of the Island in this way: 'For me the Island was a disaster in so far as I was obliged to stay there for ten years … It was brutalising. Some of the prisoners were almost impossible to live with. The guards were in many instances uncouth, near-illiterate victims of a terrible system … These negative things I try to forget. It was also an ennobling and enriching experience.' He recognises, however, that the Island has a larger role to play in national renewal: 'Robben Island was the seed-bed in which we [the political prisoners] learned that we actually need one another. It is this realisation that must form the basis of a new nation.'

Today, as a continuation of his work in the National Language Project and elsewhere, he is actively involved in fighting for the rights of the poor and oppressed in this new nation, as the head of the Workers' Organisation for Socialist Action (WOSA), founded in 1990, and Director of the Project for the Study for Alternative Education in South Africa (PRAESA) at the University of Cape Town.

James Gregory

James Gregory was a traffic officer in Worcester in 1965 when he applied to be transferred to Robben Island to work as censor for the maximum security prison. Gregory was eager to find a job which would provide free lodgings for him and his family and an opportunity for his wife to spend time at home with their children. To the prison authorities, Gregory was an attractive candidate because he could speak Xhosa and Zulu, the languages of many of the African prisoners on the Island. To these prisoners, Gregory was at first just another warder, and, worse still, a censor of their precious communications with the outside world. But later he also became, by his own account, something of an ally with them in opposing the worst excesses of the prison system.

In his autobiography, Gregory describes how initially he thought that the prisoners were all 'terrorists, who planned one day to wipe out all the white people in South Africa … They wanted to steal our lands, to rape and butcher our wives and families and to kick us into the sea…' But gradually, as he came to know the prisoners better, and to do his own research into the conditions under which black South Africans had to live, Gregory began to appreciate, if not to support, the choices these men had made to oppose apartheid. He also describes the very real trauma that the prison guards on the Island suffered, as ill-educated men facing the cream of the anti-apartheid struggle in an isolated and notorious prison. There was much bullying not only among the warders themselves but also of prisoners, and many warders drank heavily, including Gregory himself.

Gregory was transferred off the Island, at his own request, in 1975 and was employed at Pollsmoor Prison (with a brief interlude as Robben Island censor based in Cape Town) until some of the ANC and PAC leaders were sent there in 1982. He accompanied Nelson Mandela to Victor Verster Prison and remained as his personal guard until his release in 1990. They seem to have struck up something of a friendship, or at least a relationship of mutual respect. He was invited to the presidential inauguration in 1994 as a guest of Mandela. But after the release of his autobiography, in which he quoted from a letter sent by Mandela to his then wife Winnie (to which Gregory had access as censor), and made comments on conversations between Mandela and his family (at which he was present as prison warder), Gregory was rebuked by the presidential office.

Nelson Mandela

Mandela is almost too well known to write about in this book, for there have been hundreds of publications honouring his past and his present. But we can try to sketch the main details of his life and some of his experiences on the Island.

Mandela was born Rolihlahla Mandela (his clan name is Madiba) in 1918 in a small town in the Eastern Province, near Umtata. At the mission school he attended he was given the English name Nelson. He began his BA degree at Fort Hare University. After leaving university just before his final year, he worked as an articled clerk in a Johannesburg law firm and enrolled at the University of the Witwatersrand for an LL.B. During this time in Johannesburg he married his first wife Evelyn, who was to bear three of his surviving children. Her religious and apolitical lifestyle soon began to conflict with his increasingly dedicated work for the ANC and they separated in 1955. A few years later he was to marry a young woman who became just as dedicated to the ANC as he was: Nomzamo Winifred Madikizela, or Winnie.

After his trial for high treason ended in 1961, and he was released, he went underground and began to organise the military wing of the ANC, called uMkhonto weSizwe (Spear of the Nation), or MK. At this time he was dubbed the Black Pimpernel, after Baroness Orczy's character, the Scarlet Pimpernel, who boldly evaded capture during the French Revolution. On his return in 1962 from a trip to seek MK funding in the rest of Africa, he was re-arrested. As part of the five-year sentence he received, he spent two weeks on Robben Island, before the prison was fully established. On his arrival, the warders shouted, 'This is the Island. Here you will die like animals [*vrek*].' The monotony and poor conditions were somewhat relieved by the nightly gifts of sandwiches and cigarettes from a coloured warder.

Before the 1962 sentence could be completed, however, the Rivonia Trial began. The government had discovered a secret ANC headquarters, Lilliesleaf Farm, and arrested almost the entire High Command of the military wing of the ANC there. Recalled from Robben Island, Mandela was accused with the others of sabotage and conspiracy against the state. In 1964 all of them (excepting one who was acquitted and a few who jumped bail) were sentenced to life imprisonment. They were fortunate in escaping with their lives, as the maximum penalty for the offences was the death sentence. Their principled defence and the ineptitude of the prosecutor, Percy Yutar, encouraged the judge to be somewhat lenient, according to Mandela.

Yet life on Robben Island (which was to be the prison for all those sentenced except the only white Rivonia prisoner, Dennis Goldberg) was not a pleasant prospect. It had become a much tougher place in the period while Mandela had been away: the coloured warders had been removed, and the remaining warders were brutal and racist, according to several prisoner accounts. Mandela comments in his autobiography that 'journeying to Robben Island was like

going to another country'.

As prisoner 488/64, Mandela was to remain on the Island until March 1982. His attitude towards prison was that it was 'a microcosm of the struggle as a whole. We would fight inside as we had fought outside ... [just] on different terms.' The political prisoners were confronted with a loss of personal control, disorientation and isolation, arbitrary punishments, discriminatory regulations and often cruel prison authorities. The light in each cell burned all day and all night. 'Coloured', 'Indian' and African prisoners received different diets, and prisoners were further classified into A, B, C, or D categories, which carried a decreasing number of privileges. Visits by family and friends were severely restricted, as were the numbers of letters sent and received. For Mandela the only pleasing prospect of prison was that it gave him time to think and reflect. Yet the prisoners could talk to each other, while cleaning out their sanitary buckets and while working in the quarries and the courtyard. Their struggles for better conditions and privileges, such as permission to study, did achieve some success, with the help of outside pressure. Although there were generational and political tensions, the Robben Islanders were able to form personal and political ties both among themselves and between their different political organisations. They turned the maximum security prison into a university of the anti-apartheid struggle.

In 1982 Mandela was transferred with a few other prisoners to Pollsmoor Prison in the white middle-class Cape

Town suburb of Tokai. Conditions were somewhat better there but the five (later six) of them were isolated from the other prisoners on the Island, and felt their loss. Feelers were put out by the government, which was facing difficulties both within and outside the country, for a negotiated release. But Mandela held out until other political prisoners were unconditionally released. In the meantime, at Pollsmoor and (after 1988) at Victor Verster, he began negotiations with government officials, which culminated in the unbanning of the ANC, PAC and SACP in 1990. Mandela was released finally on 11 February of that year and the first democratic elections took place in April 1994. Shortly thereafter Mandela became President of South Africa.

How to get to the Island

Tickets are sold from the Embarkation Point on Jetty 1 at the V&A Waterfront, directly in front of the extension to the Victoria Wharf. The Embarkation Office is open from 07h30 to 17h00. Tickets are limited and are available on a first-come first-served basis. Because of the popularity of the tours you are advised to be at the Embarkation office early. For further information, please call (021) 419 1300 during office hours.

There are three tours daily. Ferries depart promptly at the times indicated. Please ensure that you arrive 30 minutes before departure.

	Depart Cape Town	Arrive Cape Town
Tour 1	09h30	13h00
Tour 2	11h45	14h45
Tour 3	13h15	16h45

Advance bookings can only be made by groups of 10 or more. They must be arranged and paid for at least 7 working days in advance. A list of names of passengers travelling in the group must be sent to the booking office at least 7 days in advance. Advance bookings are generally made by tour operators, companies and schools.

Group tours can be accommodated by special arrangement. Special rates are available on written request. Physically challenged visitors should inform the booking office prior to their visit.

The following labels appear on the map:

THE LIGHT HOUSE

MINTO-HILL THE HIGHEST POINT ON THE ISLAND

VAN RIEBEECK'S QUARRY

THE GUEST HOUSE THIS USED TO BE WHERE THE COMMANDER OF THE ISLAND LIVED

THE ANGLICAN CHURCH, 1841

THE OLD MALE LEPER CHURCH, BUILT IN 1895.

FAURE JETTY

(from Barbara Hutton, *Robben Island*, Sached Books, 1994)

Major Sources Consulted

Davey, A. 'Robben Island and the Military, 1931–1960', in Deacon, H. (ed.) *The Island: A History of Robben Island, 1488–1990* (Cape Town, 1996).

Davids, A. 'The History of the Karamats: The Karamat on Robben Island', *Boorhaanol Newsletter*, 26(2), n.d.

Gregory, J. *Goodbye Bafana, my Prisoner, my Friend* (London, 1995).

Huigen, S. 'Jarige Meisjes, 'Hottentotten, en het Zand van Robben Eijland: Pieter de Neyn aan de Kaap (1672–74)', *De Zeventiende Eeuw*, 7(2) (1991).

Jacobs, J.H. 'Narrating the Island: Robben Island in South African literature', *Current Writing*, 4 (1992).

Judges, S. 'Poverty, Living Conditions and Social Relations: Aspects of Life in Cape Town in the 1830s' (M.A. thesis, UCT).

Lubbe, G. 'Robben Island: The Early Years of Muslim Resistance', *Kronos*, 12 (1987).

Malherbe, V.C. 'David Stuurman: Last Chief of the 'Hottentots', *African Studies*, 39(1) (1980).

Malherbe, V.C. *Krotoa, Called Eva: a Woman Between* (Cape Town, 1990).

Mandela, N. *Long Walk to Freedom* (London, 1994).

Mostert, N. *Frontiers: An Epic of South Africa's Creation and the Tragedy of the Xhosa People* (London, 1992).

Ntloedibe, E.L. *Here is a Tree: A Political Biography of Robert Mangaliso Sobukwe* (Botswana, 1995).

Peires, J. *The Dead Will Arise* (Johannesburg, 1989).

Penn, N. 'Robben Island 1488–1805' in Deacon, H. (ed.) *The Island: A History of Robben Island, 1488–1990* (Cape Town, 1996).

Pinkerton, A.W.P. 'Introductory Lecture on Climate' (Edinburgh Medical School, Edinburgh, 1857).

Pogrund, B. *Sobukwe and Apartheid* (Johannesburg, 1990).

Riley, P. 'Conservation Survey of Robben Island' (unpublished report, National Monuments Council).

Spear, J.A. 'Cape Reactions to the Langalibalele Affair: A Study of Eastern and Western Province attitudes' (unpublished B.A. (Hons.) thesis, UCT, 1977).

Stapleton, T.J. 'Reluctant Slaughter: Rethinking Maqoma's Role in the Cattle Killing', *International Journal of African Historical Studies*, 26(2) (1993).

Stapleton, T.J. 'The memory of Maqoma: An Assessment of Jingqi Oral Tradition in Ciskei and Transkei', History in Africa, 20 (1993).

Tambo, O. *Preparing for Power* (Oxford, 1987).

Villa-Vicencio, C. *The Spirit of Freedom* (London, 1996).

Werz, B.S. and Deacon, J.C.G. 'Operation Sea Eagle: Final Report on a Survey of Shipwrecks around Robben Island' (unpublished report, National Monuments Council, 1992).